INSTAGRAM

THE ULTIMATE INSTAGRAM MARKETING GUIDE FOR BUSINESS

How to Build A Brand And Attract Followers On Instagram

by David Jones

Table of Contents

INSTAGRAM

Disclaimer

While all attempts have been made to verify the information provided in this book, the author does not assume any responsibility for errors, omissions, or contrary interpretations of the subject matter contained within. The information provided in this book is for educational and entertainment purposes only. The reader is responsible for his or her own actions and the author does not accept any responsibilities for any liabilities or damages, real or perceived, resulting from the use of this information.

Introduction

The word Instagram came from two components features; instant and telegram. Instagram is a photo and video sharing website and mobile application that allows users to upload, filter and share photos with followers and friends on Instagram and other social networking sites simultaneously.

Instagram also offers a video-sharing option allowing users to share videos of up to 15 seconds in length. Instagram today is widely used by individuals for social as well as business purposes. Businesses use Instagram to promote their products or services while connecting with their followers. And for all these reasons, as a business oriented person you need to fully capitalize on it. It provides benefits:

1) Increased Engagement. Having an active Instagram account with interesting and valuable content can earn you crazy levels of engagement with your targeted customers. Thus, you don't need to spend more time and effort to connect with your audience.

2) Free Marketing. This is one of the best benefits and the reason why you shouldn't forsake Instagram when it comes to social selling. You can showcase your services and products in a fast and easy way. It also gives you an opportunity to show off more of what you offer.

3) Increasing your Website Traffic. Even if you cannot add clickable links to each Instagram update you post, this social media platform can be an influential source of traffic.

4) Build Personality and Trust. With Instagram, you can easily create an emotional connection with your audience. It also allows you to share the day-to- day experiences of your business in a casual and informal way. Thus, it gives a personal feel to your business.

The photos on your Instagram account can make your company more trustworthy and attractive which in turn can have a positive effect on your business.

5) Update People on Your Latest Promos. With Instagram, you can share photo updates about your business quickly and easily. You just need to share the latest events or activities that are happening in your company.

6) Become More Competitive. If you are using Instagram to market your business, you can easily reach your target audience. This gives you an advantage over your competitors.

In order to connect with a specific individual or business on Instagram you will need to search for and follow them. Public profiles are easy to follow, and anyone can. However, private profiles are restricted and require permission from the profile's owner.

Instagram is relatively easy to use and allows businesses to connect with their potential customers in a visually appealing way.

Instagram offers more potential than instant photo sharing – it allows those pictures to generate customers and brand recognition.

Sharing pictures through Instagram is easier than on other social networking sites where it can take minutes to upload a single photo. Instagram on the other hand offers faster and higher quality images.

Many people capitalize on Instagram as part of a larger Internet marketing strategy.

Whether you are a website owner, fashion blogger, a logistics company, in retail, or the food industry, the evolution and popularity of Instagram provides the potential to connect and do business with hundreds, thousands and even millions of people across the globe.

Instagram encourages customer participation and enables them to connect with you on a more personal level compared to other internet marketing strategies.

Chapter 1- How Instagram Works

As mentioned previous in the book introduction, Instagram uses photo and videos to convey a message to the targeted audience and this make it to be a photo sharing site. Photo sharing has been given a major social upgrade since the introduction of Instagram. People often use this social media platform to improve their photos using special effects and cool filters before sharing them with followers and friends.

Like the thousands of businesses to date you too can start using this form of social media as an excellent way to advertise your company. Since everyone loves visual images, posting pictures of products and even personnel will make them feel closer to you.

BENEFITS OF HAVING AN ACCOUNT

To start with, many small business owners in particular at times make the mistake of promoting their business by creating personal accounts. This does very little for the credibility of your business and at the same time comes across as amateur and unprofessional.

It is alright to promote and share the photos and other content of your business by linking it on your profile but not very beneficial for your friends and family to be constantly reminded of your business via a personal page.

So make sure that you run a completely independent profile for your business on Instagram. Business and personal life should always be separated, especially when it comes to social media marketing.

Now that your business is officially on Instagram, it is time to play with it. The first thing you need to do is add a profile photo that reflects your business properly.

The profile photo can be of your latest products, your company's logo or simply a photo of your head office. Whatever works for you!

Next, add a link to your website so that those reaching out to you can easily reach out to your business too. Instagram offers biographies of up to 150 characters, which will eventually appear on your profile page. You can add a little info about the business, what you do and then add a link at the very end.

The next step should be to connect your profile to other social networking sites like Facebook and other third-party sites like Twitter, Foursquare, Hipstamatic etc. You can easily connect to these sites by going to Settings on your Android or iOS.

Device and tapping "Sharing Settings" you can then easily connect all the third party networking sites you wish to integrate.

It is essential that you connect the other networking sites in order to increase visibility and accessibility. You can also reach out to your Facebook friends on Instagram by tapping on "Find Friends."

There are plenty of ways to connect through Instagram and numerous features to try out. The best way to do that is to keep on playing with it until you understand exactly how it functions and how you can make the most of it.

INSTAGRAM FEATURES

Instagram offers numerous features that are not only a lot of fun to try out, but also help you connect with your audience. The following are some of the most beneficial features of Instagram:

Web Profile

Your business profile is the window through which followers can get an idea of exactly what it is you are trying to promote. Your profile should be regularly updated with correct information.

Hashtags

Instagram hashtags work pretty much the same way as hashtags on Twitter. They enable users to get access to desired or similar content relatively easily. All you need to do is simply start clicking photos and hash-tagging them with relative tags.

You can also add hashtags in the comment section once the picture is taken.

The following are a few rules for using hashtags: You can only tag your own pictures and videos and cannot tag others.

1. You can use a maximum of 30 tags per photo or video. If you add more than that the comment will not be posted.

2. You cannot use characters like "%" or "?" in hashtags, however, you can use numbers.

3. You can search for hashtags by tapping on Profile tab>Search Instagram>Tags.

4. Make sure that your profile settings are set on public rather than private, otherwise your photos and videos will only be available to your followers and not the rest of the Instagram community.

Follow

It is important that you set your profile to public so that it is easier for others to find and follow you.

However, don't just wait for others to follow you. You should be following other relative users and businesses in order to get a good idea of what people are talking about and what is trending.

Make sure that you follow your competitors, news channels, celebrities and other prominent and relative users.

OTHER PHOTO EDITING FEATURES

There are plenty of other photo editing features available on Instagram including Lux, which makes the picture more prominent and profound, High Dynamic Range, Light Bokeh, Auto Exposure, combining multiple images, straightening images and more.

The Web Feed

Web enables users to log in and check their news feed on a desktop or laptop computer the same way they do on their Smart phones. Instagram has been a mobile-based site for a very long time, and it still is. However, now you can access your newsfeed on any device.

Simply go to Instagram.com, log in with your details and browse through those you follow on the web in pretty much the same way you would on a smartphone.

The web feed will make it very easy for your followers to check your photos and videos on the go at their own convenience. The larger screen undoubtedly increases the visibility of your products and enables them to move from the image to your website, leads to more brand buzz

Photo Maps

Instagram also offers Photo Map that allows you to easily add the time and location of the photos you take. This option makes it very easy for businesses to let their followers know where they can be found.

For example, if you are attending a convention or trade fair then, by simply posting a picture with the location, it will be easy for others to find you. Photo Map also enables you to look at a broader picture of where your photos were mostly taken and the ability to organize photos according to their time and date.

Your followers will be able to see your photo map if you permit them to do so, allowing them to see a map of what your business has been up to at specific times.

By default, photomaps are turned off. You will have to switch on the "Add to your Photo Map" before posting a photo.

The New Instagram Video

With the introduction of the new video, you can now record up to 15 seconds of video, choose from 13 different filters and share with millions of people across the globe.

The new feature has seen a lot of positive feedback because of its ease of use and editing options. You can also choose a specific frame from the video to appear as the cover image to make it more visually appealing.

Video for Instagram also offers the Cinema feature with which you can stabilize the video once it has been made.

From a business perspective you can use this function to encourage your customers to post videos when using your products or services, or post short videos of why you love them, ask for feedback or post your own behind-the-scene videos.

The options are endless and so is the potential to communicate and connect with those who matter to you and your business.

Chapter 2- Making Use Of Instagram

Instagram is effective and productive only when it is correctly used and implemented. Simply making a profile and posting a picture or video each week will do very little to generate interest or engage followers, let alone foster sales.

It is only by posting useful content that your followers will want to click the "like" button and have enough interest to visit your website where they can convert into customers.

Instagram. Pictures can be worth a lot more than a thousand words. They can be your followers' window into your world or your door into theirs.

How to Get Followers

Your first step should be to get followers, more followers mean more potential business. Posting pictures or videos will not only give exposure to followers on Instagram, but also to those following you on other social networking sites.

Know Your Audience

You need to understand exactly who your target audience is and what they're interested in.

You have a better chance of connecting with them if you have a good idea of who they are. This is where Instagram differs in personal and business use.

When using a personal Instagram account, your objective is to let your personality show through interesting pictures, regardless whether or not anyone approves. With your business profile, it's not about what is personally relevant to you, but what is relevant to your audience.

This doesn't mean that your images or videos need to be static or boring; this simply means that you need to reflect your potential followers' preferences.

You can also get a good idea about your targeted audience by following and analyzing your competitors' Instagram pages. Go through them to see what kind of pictures and videos they have posted and what their followers are commenting.

You can also use geo-tags to see what people are posting in your area, and what seems is to be trending on social media in general.

At this point, research is paramount, and will enable you to plan your strategy accordingly.

Once you understand your audience and their preferences then start posting pictures accordingly. Simply posting images of your products or services will do very little to interest viewers.

The Power of Hashtags

Hashtags are the compass of an image or video. They are the ones that lead you to your potential consumers and lead those looking for the products and services you offer straight to your profile.

Hashtags are simple to use but quite difficult to strategize. Misleading hashtags can negatively impact the credibility of your business, whereas targeted hashtags can lead to more followers and thus more potential customers.

What Likes and Comments Can Do for You

There are about 1 billion daily "likes" on Instagram. That's a lot of likes by a lot of people. So how do you make your mark with such competition? And what good could these likes and comments do anyway?

In the easiest of terms, "likes" help build the popularity of your business and brand.

Those likes or comments are not always for the image or video, but for the personality and the desire for association. That's what your images and videos can do for you provided you give your targeted audience something to associate themselves with.

Perhaps coverage of a specific event, a shout out to a star customer or simply asking for opinions on a specific promotional campaign.

Generating likes and comments can be tricky, but also interesting and productive at the same time. Where likes can help increase popularity and association, comments can help start conversations and engagement.

Who You Need to Be Following

Followers will follow as long as you keep on adding value to their time, whether it is through a blast from the past or futuristic ideas. The trick is to keep them engaged, interested and educated.

However, Instagram is not just about increasing your number of followers, it's also about you following the right people. You will also need to start following relevant users in order to get a good idea of what the others are saying, and how you can integrate that knowledge into your own promotional strategies in Instagram and elsewhere.

You need to be following people you like as well as your competition on Instagram to get a good idea of what the world is saying. For instance, if you run an online business selling umbrellas, then you need to know the weather in your area at all times.

You also need to know what new products, services or value your competitors are offering to your potential customers.

If they are offering giveaways or discounts then are they working? Are their posts getting likes and comments? If yes, then what kind of pictures are they posting? Seeking answers to these questions will help you strategize and post pictures and videos that create customers and brand loyalty

When to Post

Timing is very important when it comes to posting on any social networking site, whether to attract new followers or engage the present ones. Posting images and videos is as much a science as it is an art.

Instagram has a life span of about 3-4 hours, which means after that it will get so lost in the newsfeed that the chances of being found will be pretty much nonexistent.

Make sure that you post at a time when there is the most traffic. Ideal times are mornings, evenings, lunch breaks and weekends. Basically – right when people get to work, when people are taking a lunch break, and when people come home from work. Many people generally use Instagram while commuting to or from work.

You can experiment by posting at different times on different days to see what generates the most feedback in terms of likes and comments. Make sure you don't post a picture every hour on the same day.

Even a great picture will seem annoying if it's too excessive. A good idea is to post around five images in a week and keep a journal of the feedback on each image. Then, change the timings the next week.

This might seem like too much work, but it's essential when it comes to knowing your potential consumers and their habits. Also make sure to keep a record of what kind of images, videos and hashtags generate the most followers, likes and comments.

Engaging in social media for business gives you an insight into your potential customers' preferences, likes and dislikes.

Chapter 3- How To Market On Instagram

Getting followers is just the first milestone. It is like convincing a shopper to stop at your window and check the display. But the display will not generate into sales if the content inside is not worth checking out.

Hence, you will need to dress it up and keep offering a variety of items and displays so the shopper remains engaged and ready to take it to the next level - sales.

Selling your products and services with the help of images and videos is not a new concept; it has been in play for a very long time, pretty much since the beginning of advertising.

Whether in newspapers or TV ads, visuals have had a major impact on consumers' decision-making, but the consumers' needs and habits are evolving, which means your strategies need to evolve too.

Instagram is that evolution, rather than knocking on a potential consumer's doorstep you invite them into your own space and then gradually turn them from followers to customers.

But that transition is not an easy one. Once you have your followers you will need to constantly keep on developing interesting visual content that targets your audience at the right time and in the right manner.

Know Your Followers and Fans

The first step will be to know your followers and fans. This might seem similar to knowing your target audience, but it differs in the sense that you need to be very specific and cater to those who have already shown interest in your brand by following you.

Be sure to research what their preferences are, what they seem to be purchasing and what kind of content they are most interested in.

Analyze which pictures and videos create the biggest ripple, what kind of posts increase your website traffic and what videos and photos your followers are talking about.

Understanding your audience is your first step to entertaining and inspiring them, so make sure that you keep a constant check through and through.

The fact that you have a decent amount of followers does not say much if they aren't interested in the content you are posting. It is only through engagement that those followers will convert, and the first step towards that is to understand them.

You need to be posting interesting photos and images, but how do you come up with content that can compete against over 40 million new pictures every day? That is a lot of pictures, but that does not mean you cannot come up with another unique one each day to engage your targeted audience with.

The following are a few tips and tricks to make your photos and videos worth a second look:

•Primarily you will need to show your products so that your followers can identify your company with the products that you promote. But these product photos or videos don't necessarily need to be boring.

•Allow your followers to see how your products are made, whether through photos or videos. Make a small video of a muffin at your coffee shop or a photo of a designer at work for your web development firm. There is a story behind every product and service, and by sharing it with your followers you will be letting them in on it.

•Show the usability of your products and services by posting pictures or videos of people using them. You can also ask your followers to share photos using a designated hashtag to do the same.

•Make your Instagram followers feel valuable. They are a special bunch that took the time out to follow you and stay updated with your posts. They need to be given attention. Offer exclusive content, or announce new offerings, deals or products on your Instagram page before it is announced elsewhere.

•Give them previews of exclusive content like a new product in the making, office renovations or even preparations for an office party. There is nothing more personal and engaging then giving your followers a sneak peek into what actually goes on behind the curtains.

•Introduce your employees. This will humanize your brand and will encourage your employees to work better knowing that they are being acknowledged and appreciated. You can also use it as an ongoing campaign to post the picture of the employee of the week or something like the best picture taken by an employee.

•Let them know where you have been, as it will help followers connect with you on a more personal level. If you have been at a trade fair, a promotional event, press conference or even at the airport, let your followers know. Make sure that you post a picture with a location and invite them to join you.

•A cute picture will almost always get a like or comment. Make sure you capitalize on it!

•Just like most forms of art, pictures and videos need to be thought provoking. Otherwise, the purpose is lost. Try to set a theme or tone with your photos. If you are keeping it light and funny, don't change the tone abruptly, or you could risk losing your followers.

What You Need to Offer

In recent years, social media has been used to promote people's businesses, this means there are plenty of businesses offering plenty of great opportunities to keep their audiences engaged and educated. You will need to fight for their attention each time you post a photo or video.

The best way to do that is to make offers that are hard to ignore and harder to refuse. Here are a few ways you can get your followers involved by offering something in return for their time and effort:

Photo Contests

Everyone loves a photo contest. You get to showcase your photography skills to a larger audience, and get rewarded for it too. Photo contests are also a good way to spike up your followers. You can ask users to post photos of themselves using your products with your company's hashtag, along with an interesting caption. Or, they can post their favorite piece of furniture, or an item that reminds them of their first pet.

The ideas are endless. Be sure to offer an attractive prize as a reward. It can be a subscription to your own services, a goody bag, tickets to a concert, or a popular product like a Smart phone or a tablet, depending on your niche, market and budget.

Photo a Day Contests

Photo a Day contests have become widely popular on Instagram. All you need to do is offer a 30-day challenge to post a picture with a different theme each day. The ideas can be as specific or as general as you'd like them to be. Simply make a thirty-day plan and post a picture of it on your blog or Instagram along with the start and end date.

There can be a theme for the whole contest such as winter. Each day can be a little more specific like Christmas, snowflakes, fireplaces, reflection, snowman etc.

You can have a random Picture Photo a Day contest as well. The closer the theme is to the industry that you cater to, the more relevant and productive the outcome.

Don't forget to offer desirable prizes and ask your followers to tag the photos appropriately.

You Don't HAVE To Give Away A Prize

You do not necessarily need to offer prizes to make your followers feel special.

Simply ask them to hashtag your product, brand or company name every time they use it, along with a good picture. Post a picture of the most interesting picture each week. Just the acknowledgment can go a long way when it comes to engagement on social media.

Unique Hashtags

Unique hashtags are another way to make lasting impressions on Instagram. Many businesses use special hashtags to promote events or new products on Instagram and on Twitter.

Chapter 4- Branding A Product

Businesses today are based as much on the quality of their products and services, as they are on branding. You might be offering awesome products, but if they are not associated with a brand, the success will be greatly limited. Branding is a long, hard and slow process, or so it was before social media.

Now, you can easily brand your business by showcasing it to your audience the way you want it to be seen, but this too will require constant efforts and strategic planning. The first step to branding your business on Instagram will be to decide how you want your targeted audience to associate with it.

Many businesses make the mistake of looking for successful recipes for branding, and so they make their business affordable and exclusive, innovative and traditional and for young and for old, all at the same time.

But that's not branding, on the contrary, that's spreading yourself too thin. You want to find a niche audience when promoting your business on Instagram.

You will need to make your photos coherent and your strategy well researched, this only means that it needs to have some association with your brand.

> ➤ Build Momentum about Your Products or Services

Followers will associate your business with a specific product or service if they already have a connection with them. A lot of businesses today start building momentum about their products or services prior to the release in order to increase followers' interest and knowledge.

You can also share pictures or videos of work in progress, or even the picture of your graphic designer with a thinking expression on and an interesting caption like "That's how he came up with the awesome idea we will announce next week."

You can also take tricky or confusing pictures or videos and ask your followers to guess what your new offering is and perhaps even offer a reward or prize to the one that gets it right.

You can also lure them into checking your website out for more exclusive content. Be sure to add a link that goes back to a specific, relevant page on your site.

➢ Asking for Feedback and Opinions

Your followers are your valued customers or potential customers, and so it is important that you make them feel special and let them know that their opinion matters. Ask them for feedback through photos and videos about their experience with your products or services.

Asking for feedback and addressing it will not only help create a bond it will also lead to more sales, and brand identification.

Chapter 5- Turning Followers Into Customers

The primary objective of using Instagram for business purposes is to eventually turn leads into sales, to make your followers your customers. It is important that your photos and videos lead your customers to your website and prompt them to subscribe to your newsletters, and download your e-books.

Your strategies need to be designed in such a manner that your videos and photos encourage the viewers to show interest in your products and services.

Call to Action

A call to action directs your followers where you want them to go, so they convert into sales. Make sure that you have a call to action along with a link. If you are posting pictures for an upcoming event, a trade fair, a new product launch or even a sunny day, tell them to see what you have to offer.

For instance, add a link to accept your invitation to a trade fair, or a link to how your products and services will compliment the weather or more information about your upcoming projects. Guide your followers and make it easy for them to find the link.

Promo Codes

Deal seekers are everywhere, and they are constantly on the lookout for the best deals in town. No longer do people spend ages looking at magazines or newspapers for coupons or discounts. Coupons have made it online, and social media in particular has become a popular spot to hunt for them.

Promo codes have become widely popular on Twitter and Instagram and many businesses are using them to keep followers wanting more.

Create images that offer exclusive coupons and discounts for any of your products and services. It is a fast way to boost sales and attract new followers. Don't forget to hashtag #promo code with each of your promotional images to increase accessibility.

Promote Latest Offers and Deals

You can easily promote your latest offers and deals on Instagram. All you need to do is take a picture of your pamphlet or promotional deal and post it on Instagram.

Make sure that you include all the information, such as the pricing or total discount along with when it will be made available.

Businesses are making new offers by the minute on social media, so people don't have enough time or patience to inquire further about them. It is ideal that you provide all the necessary information within an image to help potential customers make a quick decision.

Reply

Almost every relationship in this world is a two-way street, especially when it comes to customer relations. Simply asking your customers to post pictures, hashtag your products or services or come to your events is not enough.

It is important that you acknowledge their efforts and thank them for it. Comment on photos of consumers using your products or mentioning you, or even hash-tagging you with either positive or negative feedback.

Conclusion

No matter what type of product you are selling you should be confident that you can get your products out there in an accessible way by the use of Instagram.

This book has guided you step by step on how to setting up your own Instagram account until you are able to promote your products out there in the market.

When it comes to online businesses, most entrepreneurs use social media sites to advertise their offered products and services.

 If you want to achieve online business success, you also need to tap into this powerful tool. Among the different social media sites, Instagram will perhaps be your greatest tool.

I know you might have come acroos this phrase, "A picture is worth a thousand words " and that's the reason why you shouldn't underestimate the power of Instagram as a social media application.

Instagram can drive sales and boost correspondence just as efficiently as other social media channels. This is the high time for you take a step further and utilize this incredible social media tool.